QUILTS to Treasure

Betty Neff

Moon over MOUNTAIN
2 Public Avenue,
Montrose, PA 18801-1220
www.QuiltTownUSA.com

Introduction

My design roots began with a creative childhood. From a treadle sewing machine and paper dolls to a box of 64 crayons, (which, by the way, is still more adventuresome than a box of eight) that historical lifestyle and its documentation now play a paramount role in my work. The quilts in this book are made from fairly simple designs. By increasing the number of fabrics and colors you use, you can achieve a complex look from simple blocks!

Today you can purchase a designer collection of fabrics and it will work with these patterns. I prefer a fabric collection that is amassed over time. To achieve a broad variety you need to analyze what you already have, then decide what you need to add depth. The quilts in this book are made from fabrics

Contents

Acknowledgements

I'd like to thank my husband, Richard, for his patience and inspiration. He is my anchor. I thank my parents for a childhood of memories and for allowing me to just play, to dream and to create. A thank you to Mildred VanDyke, Arlene Martin, Joyce Zander, and The Balls Mills Quilters for their beautiful hand quilting. To my children and their spouses and my grandchildren—you have always been my "paradigm shifters" so for whatever is on the horizon, I am ready!

collected over many years. However, they would be stunning if made in Batiks, Japanese, 1930's reproductions, etc. Just expand your fabric choices enough to create your signature style. You cannot cut a kit for my quilts from five fabrics, 45 would be more appropriate. They do, however, easily lend themselves to fabric exchanges within groups.

A few working tools to consider: Backgrounds are not afterthoughts. Make them from a defined value collection. There is no "one perfect choice." Trust your senses to define acceptable. Too much fabric is not enough— meaning, I prefer several fabrics that "read" alike to one fabric used over and over. Solids can be high impact so use them sparingly, if at all. Use at least one unexpected color or fabric design for punch. Sometimes an ugly fabric is the perfect kick.

This is a special time in my life when things feel just right. I consider it a blessing to be able to share my enthusiasm with you. I hope you find inspiration for your next quilt!

Betty Neff

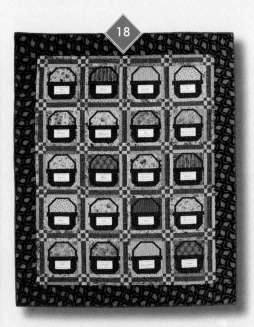

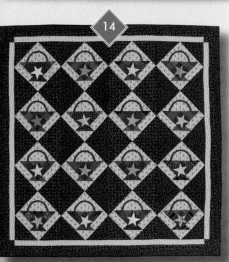

Quilt Size: 86" x 108" ❖ Block Size: 11 1/4" square

Heart and Home

Materials

- 3/4 yard dark solid for the houses
- Contrasting solid for the doors at least 8" x 12"
- 1 yard medium solid for the house background
- Assorted prints to make 6" blocks for the Houses

- Assorted light neutrals totaling at least 4 yards, for the Log Cabin blocks
- Assorted dark blue prints totaling at least 6 yards, for the Log Cabin blocks
- 1/4 yard rust for the urns
- 1/4 yard blue print for the birds

- 1/4 yard dark red print for the hearts
- 1 yard dark olive green for the vines and leaves
- 8 yards backing fabric (pieced crosswise)
- 90" x 112" piece of batting

Cutting

The appliqué patterns (pages 9 and 21) are full size and do not include a seam allowance. Make a template from each pattern. Trace around the templates on the right side of the fabrics and add a 1/4" turn-under allowance when cutting the pieces out. All other dimensions include a 1/4" seam allowance. Cut the bias strips before cutting other pieces from the green print.

For the House blocks:

- Cut 12: 3" x 3 1/2" rectangles, dark solid
- Cut 24: 1 1/4" x 4" strips, dark solid
- Cut 24: 1 1/2" squares, dark solid
- Cut 12: 2" x 4" rectangles, contrasting solid
- Cut 12: 1 1/2" x 4 1/2" strips, medium solid
- Cut 24: 1 1/2" x 2" rectangles, medium solid
- Cut 24: 2" x 12 1/2" strips, medium solid
- Cut 24: 2" x 10" strips, medium solid

NOTE: *Directions are given for three 6" (finished) block designs to be used in the House blocks. Use these or any other 6" block patterns that you like to make 12 blocks.*

For a Weathervane block:

- Cut 8: 1 1/2" x 2 1/2" rectangles, dark
- Cut 4: 1 1/2" squares, medium
- Cut 4: 1 7/8" squares, medium
- Cut 4: 1 7/8" squares, light
- Cut 12: 1 1/2" squares, light

For a Next Door Neighbor block:

- Cut 2: 3" squares, dark
- Cut 1: 2 3/8" square, dark, then cut it in half diagonally to yield 2 small triangles
- Cut 1: 4 1/4" square, medium, then cut it in quarters diagonally to yield 4 large triangles
- Cut 1: 2 3/8" square, medium, then cut it in half diagonally to yield 2 small triangles
- Cut 2: 3" squares, light
- Cut 2: 2 3/8" squares, light, then cut them in half diagonally to yield 4 triangles

For an Ohio Star block:

- Cut 2: 3 1/4" squares, dark, then cut them in quarters diagonally to yield 8 triangles
- Cut 1: 3 1/4" square, medium, then cut it in

(continued on page 6)

*My husband claimed **"Heart and Home"** as I was making the Log Cabin blocks. He likes these colors and he helped choose the pineapple, a favorite motif of ours, for the appliqué. Use any 6" block design you like for the house blocks to give your quilt your own style. Heart and Home was hand quilted by The Balls Mills Quilters.*

(continued from page 4)
quarters diagonally to yield 4 triangles
- Cut 1: 2 1/2" square, different medium
- Cut 4: 2 1/2" squares, light
- Cut 1: 3 1/4" square, light, then cut it in quarters diagonally to yield 4 triangles

For the Log Cabin blocks:
- Cut 51: 1 3/4" squares, medium solid
- Cut 1 1/2"-wide strips from the assorted darks blue prints and light neutrals

> **TIP:** Cut 2"-wide strips for the 4 outer logs. After completing the blocks, press, then trim them to 11 3/4" square.

For the Appliqué:
- Cut 4: 3/4" x 50" bias strips, green print
- Cut 1: pineapple top, green print
- Cut 26: leaves, green print
- Cut 1: pineapple, gold
- Cut 14: hearts, red print
- Cut 2 and 2 reversed: birds, blue print
- Cut 2: vases, dark gold

Also:
- Cut 11: 2 1/2" x 40" strips, dark print, for the binding

Directions

For a Weathervane block:
1. Draw a diagonal line from corner to corner on the wrong side of each 1 7/8" light square and eight 1 1/2" light squares.
2. Place a marked 1 7/8" square on a 1 7/8" medium square, right sides together. Sew 1/4" away from the drawn line on both sides. Make 4.
3. Cut the squares on the drawn lines to yield 8 pieced squares. Press the seam allowances toward the medium fabric.
4. Lay out a 1 1/2" medium square, 1 1/2" light square, and 2 pieced squares. Sew them together to make a corner unit. Make 4.

5. Place a marked 1 1/2" light square on a 1 1/2" x 2 1/2" dark rectangle, right sides together. Sew on the drawn line.

6. Press the square toward the corner, aligning the edges. Trim the seam allowances to 1/4".
7. Place a marked square on the opposite end of the rectangle. Sew on the marked line. Press and trim, as before, to complete a Flying Geese unit. Make 4.

8. Sew a Flying Geese unit to a 1 1/2" x 2 1/2" dark rectangle. Make 4.

9. Lay out the corner units, Flying Geese units, and the 2 1/2" medium square. Sew them into rows and join the rows to complete a Weathervane block.

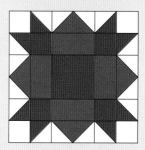

For a Next Door Neighbor block:
1. Sew a small dark triangle to a small medium-value triangle. Make 2. Sew the units together to make an Hour Glass unit. Set it aside.

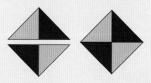

2. Make 4 pieced squares as described in Steps 1 through 3 of the Weathervane block directions, using the 3" dark squares and 3" light squares.
3. Lay out the Hour Glass unit, pieced squares, large medium-value triangles, and the small light triangles. Sew them into diagonal sections, as shown. Sew the

sections together to complete a Next Door Neighbor block.

For an Ohio Star block:

1. Sew a dark triangle to a light triangle to make a pieced triangle. Make 4. Sew a dark triangle to a medium triangle to make a pieced triangle. Make 4.

2. Sew a dark/light pieced triangle to a dark/medium pieced triangle to make an Hour Glass unit.

3. Lay out the Hour Glass units, 2 1/2" light squares, and the 2 1/2" medium square. Sew them into rows and join the rows to complete an Ohio Star block.

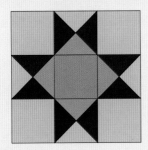

For the House blocks:

1. Lay out two 1 1/2" x 2" medium solid rectangles, two 1 1/2" dark solid squares, and a 1 1/2" x 4 1/2" medium solid strip. Sew them together to make a chimney section.

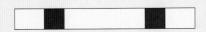

2. Sew two 1 1/4" x 4" strips to a 2" x 4" dark solid rectangle. Sew a 3" x 3 1/2" dark solid rectangle to the top to complete the door unit. Make 12.

3. Trace the Roof foundation 12 times on the foundation paper.

4. Piece each Roof foundation using the following fabrics in these positions:

    1, 2 - dark solid

    3, 4 - medium solid

5. Trim the fabric 1/4" beyond the edges of the foundations.

6. Sew a chimney section to a roof section. Sew a door section to a 6" block. Join the top and bottom to make a House block. Make 12.

7. Sew 2" x 10" medium solid strips to the sides of a block. Trim the excess. Press the seam allowances toward the strips.

8. Sew 2" x 12 1/2" medium solid strips to the top and bottom of the block. Press, as before. Repeat for the remaining blocks.

9. Trim each block to 11 3/4" square.

For the Log Cabin A blocks:

1. Sew a 1 3/4" medium solid square to a 1 1/2"-wide light strip. Add another square right after the first one. Continue in this manner until the entire strip is filled. Continue adding squares to other light strips until you've sewn 40 squares.

2. Cut the strips between the squares. Press the seam allowances away from the center square. Stack the units right side up with the light square toward the bottom.

3. Sew a pieced unit to a 1 1/2" light strip. Continue adding pieced units to that strip and others until you've sewn 40.

4. Cut the strips between the units. Press the seam allowances away from the center square. Stack the units wrong side up with the last strip added toward the bottom.

5. Sew a pieced unit to a 1 1/2" dark strip. Continue as before until you've sewn 40.

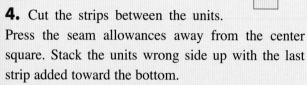
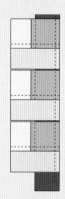

6. Cut the strips between the units and press as before.

7. Sew a dark strip to the remaining side of each unit in the same manner.

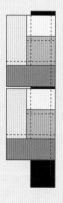

8. Continue adding light and dark strips to each block in a clockwise direction until each side has 5 logs. NOTE: *If you cut 2" strips, use them for the outer logs. Press the blocks then trim them to 11 3/4" square.*

Block A

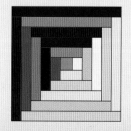

9. Referring to the following diagrams, make 2 Block B's, 4 Block C's, 1 Block D, and 4 Block E's.

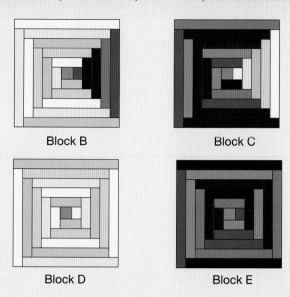

Block B   Block C

Block D   Block E

10. Referring to the photo on page 5, lay out the blocks in 9 rows of 7. Sew the blocks into rows and join the rows.

For the Border:

1. Sew ten 1 1/2" x 40" dark print strips together to make a panel. Make 4.

2. Cut nine 4" sections from each panel.

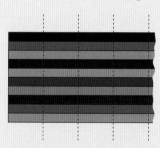

3. Join 10 sections to make a border. Make 2.

4. Measure the length of the quilt. Sew the borders to the long sides of the quilt, adjusting the length of the borders if necessary, by adding or removing a strip.

5. Join 8 sections to make a border. Make 2. Sew the borders to the top and bottom of the quilt, adjusting the length if necessary.

For the appliqué:

1. Referring to the photo, pin the pineapple top, pineapple leaves and heart to the center block of the quilt. Appliqué them in place in the same order.

2. Pin the vases to the quilt. Appliqué them in place.

Reverse appliqué the diamond shape in the center of each vase, clipping to the dots as necessary.

3. Press each 3/4" x 50" green print bias strip in thirds, wrong side in.

4. Appliqué the remaining pieces to the quilt in this order: vine, hearts, birds, and leaves.

Finishing

1. Finish the quilt according to the *General Directions*, using the 2 1/2" x 40" dark strips for the binding.

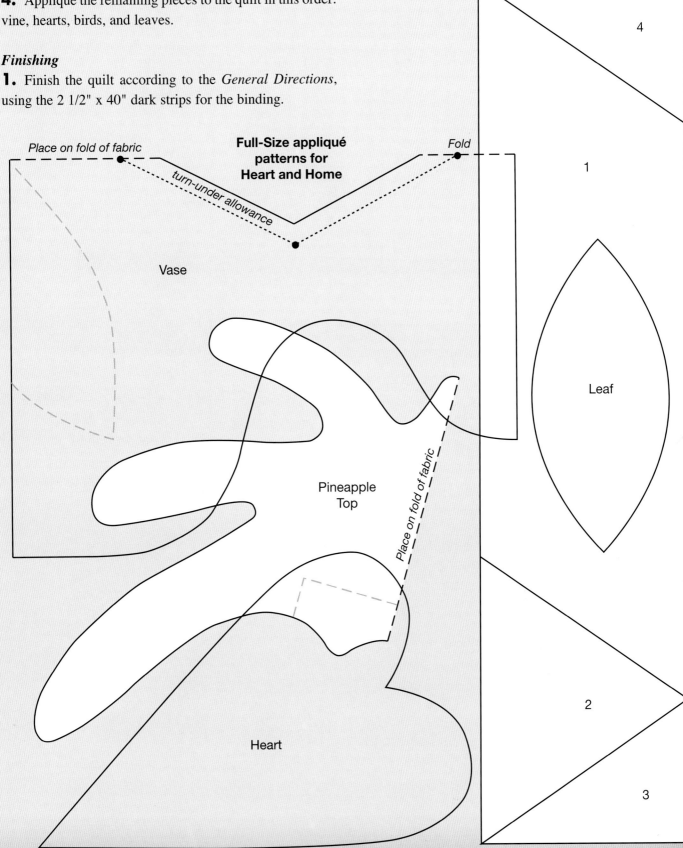

Place on fold of fabric

Full-Size appliqué patterns for Heart and Home

Fold

turn-under allowance

Vase

Full-Size Roof foundation pattern for Heart and Home

4

1

Leaf

Pineapple Top

Place on fold of fabric

Heart

2

3

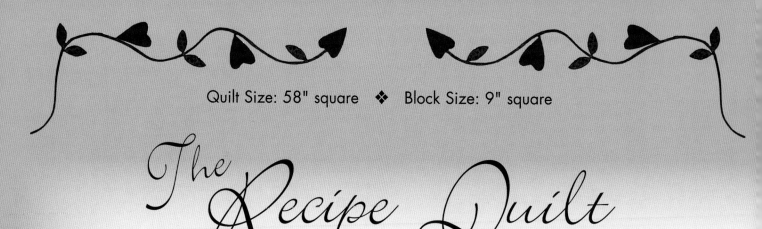

Quilt Size: 58" square ❖ Block Size: 9" square

The Recipe Quilt

Materials

- Assorted red prints, each at least 9" square
- 1 1/8 yards yellow print
- 1 1/2 yards green print

- 1/4 yard muslin
- 1/4 yard red print for the cornerstones

- 1 3/4 yards tan plaid
- 3 1/2 yards of light solid backing fabric
- 62" square of batting

Cutting

Dimensions include a 1/4" seam allowance.

For each of 16 blocks:
- Cut 4: 2" x 3 1/2" strips, one red print
- Cut 4: 2 5/8" squares, same red print

Also:
- Cut 16: 3 1/2" squares, muslin
- Cut 128: 2 1/2" squares, yellow print, then cut them in half diagonally to yield 256 triangles
- Cut 64: 2" x 3 1/2" strips, yellow print
- Cut 7: 2 1/2" x 40" strips, green print, for the binding
- Cut 40: 2 3/4" x 9 1/2" strips, green print
- Cut 25: 2 3/4" squares, red print, for the cornerstones
- Cut 2: 6" x 60" lengthwise strips, tan plaid
- Cut 2: 6" x 50" lengthwise strips, tan plaid

Directions

For each block:

1. Sew 2 yellow print triangles to opposite sides of a 2 5/8" red print square. Press the seam allowances toward the triangles.

2. Sew 2 yellow triangles to the remaining sides and press as before. Make 4. Trim the squares to 3 1/2", if necessary.

3. Sew a 2" x 3 1/2" red print strip to a 2" x 3 1/2" yellow print strip. Make 4.

4. Lay out the pieced units and a 3 1/2" muslin square. Sew them into rows and join the rows to complete the block. Make 16.

5. Using a fine point permanent marker, write a favorite recipe on the muslin square of each block.

(continued on page 17)

Upon completing this quilt top with reproduction fabrics, I was suddenly reminded of grandmother's kitchen and wood cookstove. So in the center of each Rolling Stone block, I wrote a recipe from my family's collection. Measurements inscribed include a "walnut-size of butter" and "teacup of sugar." **"The Recipe Quilt"** was specially hand quilted by Mildred Van Dyke.

Salad Dressing Chocolate Cake

2 cups flour
2 tsp. soda
1 cup sugar
4 tbsp. cocoa
½ tsp. salt
Sift all together then add:
½ cup Salad Dressing
1 tsp. vanilla
1 cup hot water
Beat smooth...
Betty Edwards Neff
9## — a Family Favorite!

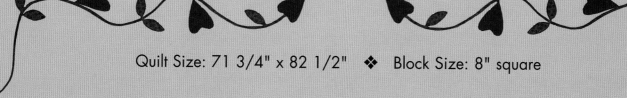

Quilt Size: 71 3/4" x 82 1/2" ❖ Block Size: 8" square

Settler's Star

Materials

- 24 dark prints for the stars, each at least 10" square
- 24 light prints for the backgrounds, each at least 10" square
- 2 yards dark brown print

- 2 yards medium brown print for the setting triangles
- 1/2 yard tan print
- 3 yards flame stitch print for the border NOTE: *If*

your fabric is non-directional, you will only need 2 1/8 yards
- 3/4 yard brown print for the binding
- 5 yards backing fabric
- 76" x 87" piece of batting

Cutting

Dimensions include a 1/4" seam allowance.

For each of 24 Star blocks:
- Cut 1: 4 1/2" square, dark print
- Cut 8: 2 1/2" squares, same dark print
- Cut 4: 2 1/2" x 4 1/2" rectangles, one light print
- Cut 4: 2 1/2" squares, same light print

Also:
- Cut 8: 1 3/4" x 70" strips, dark brown print
- Cut 2: 1 3/4" x 62" strips, dark brown print
- Cut 10: 12 5/8" squares, medium brown print, then cut them in quarters diagonally to yield 40 setting triangles
- Cut 8: 6 5/8" squares, medium brown print, then cut them in half diagonally to yield 16 corner triangles
- Cut 6: 2" x 40" strips, tan print
- Cut 4: 6 1/2" x 40" crosswise strips, flame stitch print NOTE: *Cut these before cutting the lengthwise strips. If using a non-directional print, cut two 6 1/2" x 73" lengthwise strips instead.*
- Cut 2: 6 1/2" x 72" lengthwise strips, flame stitch print
- Cut 9: 2 1/2" x 40" strips, brown print, for the binding

Directions

For each Star block:

1. Draw a diagonal line from corner to corner on the wrong side of each 2 1/2" dark print square.

2. Place a marked square on one end of a 2 1/2" x 4 1/2" light print rectangle, right sides together. Sew on the drawn line.

3. Press the square toward the corner, aligning the edges. Trim the seam allowance to 1/4".

4. Place a marked square on the opposite end of the rectangle. Stitch on the drawn line.

5. Press and trim, as before, to complete a star point unit. Make 4.

6. Lay out the 4 1/2" dark print square, the star point units, and the 2 1/2" light print squares.

7. Sew them into rows and join the rows to complete a block. Make 24.

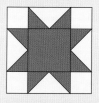

(continued on page 17)

Challenging myself to use lots of large prints in a style reminiscent of an early 1800's quilt, I designed "Settler's Star."
I made the first few blocks in a Barbara Brackman workshop and went on to set them in a strippy setting, also common
during that time period. This quilt was beautifully hand quilted by Arlene Martin.

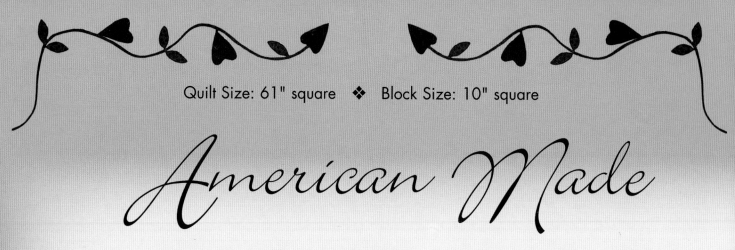

American Made

Materials

- Assorted blue prints for the baskets
- 1/4 yard blue print for the handles
- Assorted light prints for the stars
- 1 1/4 yards light print for the block backgrounds
- 1 3/4 yards red print
- 1 3/4 yards blue print
- 3/4 yard yellow print
- 3/4 yard stripe for the binding
- 3 3/4 yards backing fabric
- 65" square of batting

Cutting

Fabric for foundation piecing will be cut as you stitch the blocks. Each piece should be at least 1/2" larger on all sides than the section it will cover. Refer to the General Directions *as needed. All other dimensions include a 1/4" seam allowance. Cut lengthwise strips before cutting other pieces from the same yardage.*

- Cut 32: 2 1/2" squares, assorted blue prints, in 16 matching pairs
- Cut 48: 2 7/8" squares, assorted blue prints, then cut them in half diagonally to yield 96 triangles
- Cut 16: 1" x 10" bias strips, blue print, for the handles

From the light background print:
- Cut 8: 9" squares, then cut them in half diagonally to yield 16 large triangles
- Cut 8: 4 7/8" squares, then cut them in half diagonally to yield 16 small triangles
- Cut 32: 2 1/2" x 6 1/2" strips

From the red print:
- Cut 4: 2" x 58" lengthwise strips
- Cut 3: 15 1/2" squares, then cut them in quarters diagonally to yield 12 setting triangles
- Cut 4: 8" squares, then cut them in half diagonally to yield 8 corner triangles
- Cut 20: 2" squares

From the blue print:
- Cut 4: 2" x 58" lengthwise strips
- Cut 3: 15 1/2" squares, then cut them in quarters diagonally to yield 12 setting triangles
- Cut 4: 8" squares, then cut them in half diagonally to yield 8 corner triangles
- Cut 16: 2 1/2" squares

From the yellow print:
- Cut 8: 2" x 29 1/4" strips, yellow print

From the stripe:
- Cut 2 1/2"-wide bias strips to total at least 260" when joined for the binding

Directions

For the foundation-pieced stars:
Follow the foundation-piecing instructions in the General Directions *to piece the blocks.*

1. Trace the full size patterns (page 16) 16 times each on the foundation paper, transferring all lines and numbers. Cut each one out on the outer line.

2. Make one each of Foundations A, B, and C for each block using the same prints. Piece each foundation in numerical order using the following fabrics in these positions:

For each Foundation A:
1 - light print

(continued on page 16)

I encourage my students to
use documentation fabrics in their quilts
because I believe that the fabric documents the era,
not just the year. A millenium fabric is the perfect
background in **"American Made."** Foundation-
pieced star blocks in the baskets help to complete
the patriotic theme of my 4th of July quilt. It was
expertly hand quilted by Joyce Zander.

(continued from page 14)

2, 3 - blue print

For each Foundation B:

1 - blue print

2, 3 - light print

For each Foundation C:

1 - light print

2, 3 - blue print

3. Trim the fabric 1/4" beyond the edges of each foundation.

4. Sew a Foundation A, a Foundation B, and a Foundation C together to make a star block. Make 16.

For the Basket blocks:

1. Press the long edges of each 1" x 10" blue print bias strip 1/4" toward the wrong side.

2. Fold a large light print triangle in half and pinch the fold to mark the center. Measure 2 7/8" from the crease in both directions and make marks near the edge.

Foundation C

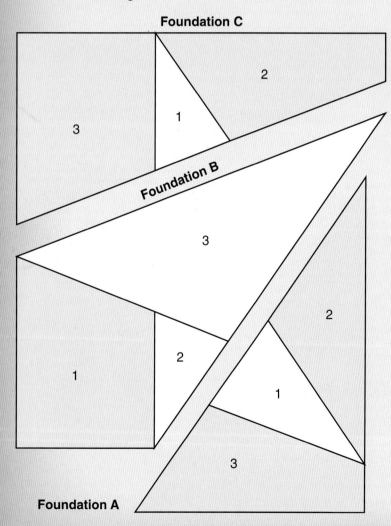

Foundation B

Foundation A

3. Pin a pressed bias strip to the triangle, aligning the inner edge of the strip with the marks on the triangle. Appliqué the strip to the triangle. Make 16.

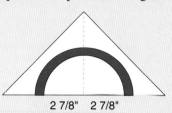

2 7/8"   2 7/8"

4. Sew 2 blue print triangles to a 2 1/2" blue print square to make a pieced triangle. Make 2 using matching prints but switch the positions of the triangles. Make 16 pairs.

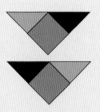

5. Sew 2 matching pieced triangles to a star block. Sew a handle unit to the Star unit. Make 16.

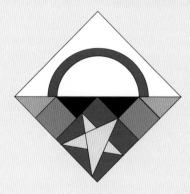

6. Sew a blue print triangle to a 2 1/2" x 6 1/2" light print strip. Make 16 and 16 reversed, as shown.

7. Sew 2 strip units to a basket unit. Sew a small light print triangle to the bottom to complete a block. Make 16.

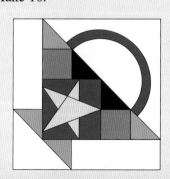

Assembly

1. Lay out 4 blocks, 6 red setting triangles, and 4 red corner triangles. Sew them into a row. Make 2 red rows and 2 blue rows.

2. Sew the rows together.

3. Sew five 2" red print squares and four 2" blue print squares together to make a Nine Patch. Make 4.

4. Sew two 2" x 29 1/4" yellow strips together, end to end. Make 4.

5. Join a yellow strip, a red strip, and a blue strip to make a border. Make 4.

6. Measure the length and width of the quilt. Trim the borders to that measurement. Sew 2 borders to opposite sides of the quilt.

7. Sew the Nine Patches to the ends of the remaining borders. Sew the borders to the top and bottom of the quilt.

8. Finish the quilt as described in the *General Directions*, using the 2 1/2"-wide stripe strips for the binding.

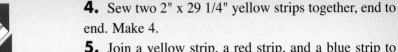

The Recipe Quilt

(continued from page 10)

Assembly

1. Lay out the blocks in 4 rows of 4.

2. Place 2 3/4" x 9 1/2" green print strips between the blocks and at the end of each row. Sew the blocks and strips into rows.

3. Sew five 2 3/4" red print squares and four 2 3/4" x 9 1/2" green print strips together alternately to make a sashing strip. Make 5.

4. Join the rows and sashing strips.

5. Measure the length of the quilt. Trim the 6" x 50" tan plaid strips to that measurement. Sew them to opposite sides of the quilt.

6. Measure the width of the quilt. Trim the 6" x 60" tan plaid strips to that measurement. Sew them to the remaining sides of the quilt.

7. Finish the quilt as described in the *General Directions*, using the 2 1/2" x 40" green print strips for the binding.

8. Write other favorite recipes and cooking-related quotes and tips on the back of the quilt.

Settler's Star

(continued from page 12)

Assembly

1. Referring to the photo on page 13, lay out the blocks on point in 4 rows of 6. Place the setting triangles beside the blocks and the corner triangles at the ends.

2. Sew the triangles to the blocks to make 4 vertical rows.

3. Sew two 2" x 40" tan print strips together, end to end, matching the design if necessary. Make 3. Trim them to 70".

4. Sew two 1 3/4" x 70" dark brown print strips to a pieced tan print strip. Press the seam allowances toward the tan strips. Make 3.

5. Measure the length of the block rows. Trim the pieced strips and the remaining 1 3/4" x 70" dark brown print strips to that measurement.

6. Sew the block rows and pieced strips together alternately. Sew the trimmed brown print strips to the left and right sides.

7. Measure the width of the quilt. Trim the 1 3/4" x 62" dark brown print strips to that measurement. Sew them to the top and bottom of the quilt.

8. Measure the length of the quilt. Trim the 6 1/2" x 72" lengthwise flame stitch strips to that measurement. Sew them to the sides of the quilt.

9. Carefully matching the design, sew 2 crosswise flame stitch strips together to make a border strip. Make 2.

10. Measure the width of the quilt. Trim the borders strips to that measurement and sew them to the top and bottom of the quilt.

11. Finish the quilt as described in the *General Directions*, using the 2 1/2" x 40" brown print strips for the binding.

Shaker Baskets

Materials

- 1/2 yard muslin
- 10 fat quarters (18" x 20") background prints (each one will make 2 blocks)
- 1 3/4 yards light print for the sashing (or seven 1/4 yard pieces for a scrappy look)

- 1 1/4 yards first purple for the sashing
- 2 1/2 yards second purple for the border
- 1 1/2 yards dark print for the baskets

- 3/4 yard dark gold for the binding
- 5 yards backing fabric
- 75" x 88" piece of batting
- Black Micron pigma pens sizes .05, .03 and .01

Cutting

Dimensions include a 1/4" seam allowance.

From the muslin:
- Cut 20: 3" x 5 1/2" rectangles (Ink the name of an herb on each one as described on page 21)

From each background-print fat quarter:
- Cut 2: 4 1/2" x 8 1/2" rectangles
- Cut 4: 2" squares
- Cut 4: 1" x 4 3/4" strips
- Cut 4: 1" x 3" strips
- Cut 2: 4" squares, then cut them in half diagonally to yield 4 triangles

From the basket fabric:
- Cut 20: 2 1/4" x 5 1/2" strips
- Cut 40: 2 1/2" x 4 3/4" strips
- Cut 20: 1 3/4" x 10 1/2" strips
- Cut 40: 1" x 7" strips
- Cut 20: 1" x 5" strips
- Cut 40: 1" x 3" strips

From the first purple print:
- Cut 15: 2" x 44" width-of-fabric strips
- Cut 6: 1 1/2" x 44" width-of-fabric strips

From the second purple print:
- Cut 2: 7" x 83" lengthwise strips
- Cut 2: 7" x 72" lengthwise strips

From the light print sashing fabrics:
- Cut 30: 1 1/2" x 44" width-of-fabric strips
- Cut 3: 2" x 44" width-of-fabric strips

From the dark gold:
- Cut 9: 2 1/2" x 40" strips, for the binding

Directions

For each Basket block:

1. Sew a 2 1/4" x 5 1/2" basket strip to the bottom of an inked muslin rectangle. Sew 2 1/2" x 4 3/4" basket strips to the sides.

2. Draw a diagonal line from corner to corner on the wrong side of two 2" background squares. Place the squares on the lower corners of the unit and sew on the lines. Press the squares toward the corners, aligning the edges. Trim the seam allowances to 1/4".

(continued on page 20)

I designed **"Shaker Baskets"** to use an assortment of purple prints and inked the names of healing herbs on each basket for continuity. A variety of background and sashing prints emphasizes my fondness for scrappy-style quilts. Try my inking technique with my tips on page 21. Quilted by Arlene Martin.

(continued from page 18)

3. Sew 1" x 4 3/4" background strips to the sides. Sew a 1 3/4" x 10 1/2" basket strip to the top to complete the basket section.

4. Measure 2 3/8" in each direction from the top corners of a 4 1/2" x 8 1/2" background rectangle. Make small marks on the edge of the fabric. Trim the corners of the rectangle from dot to dot. Discard the triangles.

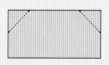

5. Sew 1" x 3" basket strips to the sides of the trimmed rectangle. Center and sew a 1" x 5" basket strip to the top. Press the seam allowances toward the basket fabric. Trim the ends of the strips even with the angled edges of the basket piece, as shown.

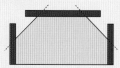

6. Center and sew 1" x 7" basket strips to the angled edges. Trim the ends of the strips. Sew 1" x 3" background strips to the sides. Trim.

7. Sew background triangles to the top corners to complete the handle section. Join the handle section and the basket section to complete the block. Make 20.

8. Trim the corner triangles if necessary to square each block to 10 1/2".

For the sashing:

1. Sew two 1 1/2" x 44" light print sashing strips to a 2" x 44" first purple strip. Make 15. Press the seam allowances toward the purple.

2. Cut forty-nine 10 1/2" sections from 13 of the pieced strips.

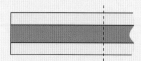

3. Cut thirty 2" sections from the remaining pieced strips. Set them aside.

4. Sew two 1 1/2" x 44" first purple strips to a 2" x 44" light print sashing strip. Press the seam allowances toward the purple. Make 3.

5. Cut sixty 1 1/2" sections from the pieced strips.

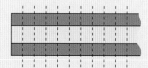

6. Join one 2" section from the first group and two sections from the second group to make a Nine Patch. Make 30.

Assembly

1. Referring to the photo on page 9, lay out the blocks in 5 rows of 4. Place sashing strips and Nine Patches between the blocks and around the edge of the layout.

2. Sew the Nine Patches and horizontal sashing strips into rows.

3. Sew the blocks and vertical sashing strips into rows.

4. Join the rows.

5. Measure the length of the quilt. Trim the 7" x 83" second purple strips to that measurement. Sew them to the sides of the quilt.

6. Measure the width of the quilt, including the borders. Trim the 7" x 72" second purple strips to that measurement. Sew them to the top and bottom of the quilt.

7. Finish the quilt as described in the *General Directions*, using the 2 1/2" x 40" dark gold strips for the binding.

Inking Tips for Bold Lettering

This "engraving" style of lettering is designed to use with a large print. It works well for inking that you want to see from a distance such as months, names, herbs, virtues, the alphabet, etc. You can also apply this technique to drawings. Follow these simple guidelines to ink the herb names on Shaker Baskets (page 18).

Materials

- Choose a tightly-woven muslin, 200-count cotton, or even a light print that allows the inking to show.
- Use a colorfast, fabric-safe waterproof pen (I suggest Micron). Sizes .05, .03, and .01 are the sizes I most frequently use. Experiment to find pens that suit your fabric and personal "hand pressure."
- A light box or other light source is usually necessary unless the fabric is light enough to see the pattern through.

Lettering

- For computer users, select a size and style of font that you like. I recommend that you find a font that is similar to your own handwriting as it will be more natural for you to reproduce. I prefer flowing script-like lettering in a font size 36 or larger.
- For non-computer users, I suggest using your own handwriting which will truly personalize your work. Children, grandchildren, and others close to you will recognize your style. Practice writing on a piece of paper the size of the area you wish to ink. You might need to make several practice pieces before you get the lettering and spacing just right. For inspiration I sometimes examine advertising layouts.

Procedure

- Center the pattern on the light box or clipboard and secure it with masking tape. Using a .01 pen, outline letters that are thick. Remove the fabric from the light source. With a .05 pen begin to fill in the letters with slanted lines. Try to keep the spacing between the lines consistent. Practice with different size pens until you find what works for you. Have fun inking!

Parsley

Chives

Full-Size appliqué patterns for Heart and Home *(Pattern begins on page 4.)*

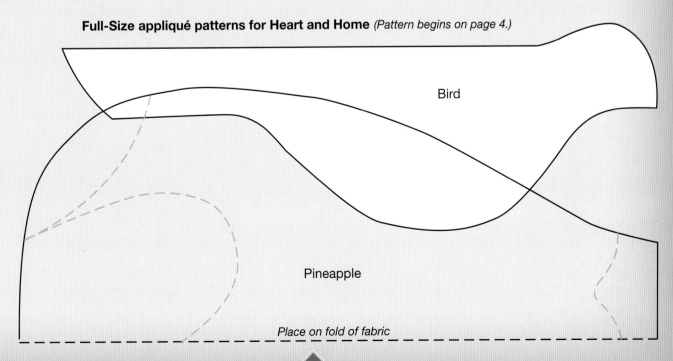

Bird

Pineapple

Place on fold of fabric

Quilt Size: 36" square ❖ Block Size: 9" square

North Country Star

Materials

- 32 medium and dark prints, each at least 2 1/4" x 17"
- 16 light prints for the blocks, each at least 2 1/4" x 17"
- 16 light prints for the background, each at least 7" x 12"
- 1/2 yard stripe for the binding
- 1 1/4 yards backing fabric
- 40" square of batting

Cutting

Dimensions include a 1/4" seam allowance.

From each medium and dark print:
- Cut 2: 1 1/8" x 17" strips

From each light print for the blocks:
- Cut 2: 1 1/8" x 17" strips

From each light background print:
- Cut 4: 3 3/8" squares
- Cut 1: 5 1/4" square, then cut it in quarters diagonally to yield 4 triangles

From the stripe:
- Cut 2 1/2"-wide bias strips to total at least 155" when joined for the binding

Directions

For each block:

1. Sew two 1 1/8" x 17" medium or dark strips to a light strip to make a panel. Make 2 using the same prints. Press the seam allowances open.

2. Trim one end of each panel at a 45° angle, as shown.

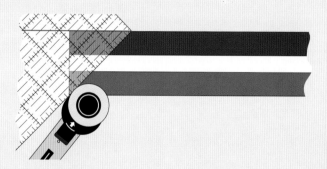

3. Measure 2 3/8" from the angled edge and cut a diamond. Cut 4 diamonds from each panel.

4. Sew 2 diamonds together, stitching only between the seam allowances and backstitching at each end. Make 4 pairs. Pay careful attention to the direction of the strips in each diamond. *(continued on page 27)*

I designed **"North Country Star"** crib quilt to commemorate the years my family lived in Pennsylvania's mountainous Cameron County where we lived closer to the stars! Most of the background of this borderless design is made from reproduction fabrics. I like to add a vintage fabric in my projects just to give the work 'an anchor' in tradition. Quilted by Joyce Zander.

Crazy Baskets

Materials

- Assorted medium and dark print scraps for the baskets
- 25 assorted medium and dark prints, each at least 6" square
- Assorted shirting prints totaling at least 1 1/2 yards
- 1 3/4 yards shirting print for the border

- 1/4 yard black print for the basket handles and bases
- 1 yard second black print for the stems and binding
- Assorted green print scraps for the leaves
- Red print for the cherries at least 10" square

- 1/2 yard red print for the cording
- 3 1/2 yards backing fabric
- 62" square of batting
- Green embroidery floss
- Lightweight paper for the basket foundations

Cutting

Dimensions include a 1/4" seam allowance. Cutting for the basket foundations will be cut as you piece the foundations.

For each of 25 Puss in the Corner blocks:
- Cut 1: 3 1/2" square, medium or dark print
- Cut 4: 2" squares, same print
- Cut 4: 2" x 3 1/2" rectangles, one shirting print

For each of 16 basket blocks:
- Cut 1: 5 1/2" square, shirting print, then cut it in half diagonally to yield 2 large triangles. You will use one.
- Cut 1: 4" square, same shirting print, then cut it in half to yield 2 small triangles. You will use one.
- Cut 2: 2" x 3 1/2" rectangles, same shirting print

Also:
- Cut 16: 1 1/8" x 6" bias strips, black print, for the basket handles
- Cut 16: 2 3/8" squares, black print, then cut them in half diagonally to yield 32 triangles
- Cut 2 1/2"-wide bias strips, second black print, to total approximately 240" when joined end to end,

for the binding
- Cut 4: 9 3/4" squares, assorted shirting prints, then cut them in quarters diagonally to yield 16 setting triangles
- Cut 2: 5 1/4" squares, assorted shirting prints, then cut them in half diagonally to yield 4 corner triangles
- Cut 2: 8" x 60" lengthwise strips, shirting print, for the border
- Cut 2: 8" x 44" lengthwise strips, shirting print, for the border
- Cut 7/8"-wide bias strips, red print, to total approximately 240" when joined end to end, for the cording

For the appliqués:
- Cut 4: 1 1/8" x 26" bias strips, green print
- Cut 4: 1 1/8" x 12" bias strips, green print
- Cut 120: leaves of various sizes, assorted green prints

NOTE: *Enlarge the border design (inside back cover) by 200% and make templates from the leaf patterns*

(continued on page 26)

I used whatever scraps of reproduction fabrics I had on hand to foundation piece the blocks in *"Crazy Baskets"*. My over-abundant collection of shirtings defined the background. Hand quilted by Joyce Zander.

(continued from page 24)
and a circle template for the cherries.
- Cut 80: cherries, red print

Directions

For the baskets:

1. Trace the basket triangle pattern (inside back cover) 16 times on paper and cut them out. Place a scrap of print fabric right side up on a paper triangle, starting either at one corner or in the middle. NOTE: *Fabrics placed near the edges of the paper should always extend at least 1/4" past the edge of the paper. Place another scrap on the first one, right sides together and aligning the edges.*

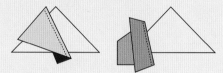

2. Sew the scraps together through the paper. Finger press the second scrap open.

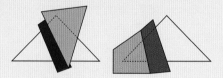

3. Sew another scrap to the second one in the same manner.

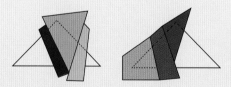

4. Continue adding scraps until the entire paper triangle is covered. Make 16. Try to vary the size and position of the scraps so the baskets will be different. Lightly press the pieced triangles on the fabric side.

5. Turn each finished foundation over and trim the fabric 1/4" beyond the edge of the paper. Set them aside.

6. Press each 1 1/8" x 6" black print bias strip in thirds, right side out. Trim each long edge leaving a 1/8" allowance.

7. Pin a pressed bias strip on a large shirting triangle, placing the ends 3 1/4" apart and forming a gentle curve. Appliqué the strip in place.

8. Center and sew the appliquéd triangle to a basket foundation. Press the seam allowance toward the basket.

9. Sew a black triangle to a 2" x 3 1/2" shirting rectangle. Make one of each as shown. Press the seam allowances open.

10. Sew the units to the basket unit. Press toward the basket. Sew a small shirting triangle to the bottom and press toward the basket to complete the block. Make 16. Trim the blocks to 6 1/2" square if necessary.

For the Puss in the Corner blocks:

1. Lay out a 3 1/2" print square, four 2" print squares, and four 2" x 3 1/2" shirting rectangles. Sew the units into 3 sections then join them to make a block. Make 25.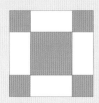

Assembly

1. Referring to the photo on the back cover, lay out the basket blocks, the Puss in the Corner blocks, and the setting and corner triangles.

2. Sew the blocks and triangles into diagonal rows and join the rows.

3. Measure the length of the quilt. Trim the 8" x 44" shirting strips to that measurement and sew them to the sides of the quilt.

4. Measure the width of the quilt, including the borders. Trim the 8" x 60" shirting strips to that measurement and sew them to the top and bottom of the quilt.

For the Appliqué:

1. Enlarge the border appliqué designs on the inside back cover by 200%. Trace the designs on paper with a permanent marker. You'll need to flip the corner design on the dashed line to make a complete pattern.

2. Place the quilt on top of the border design patterns and lightly trace them onto the quilt with a pencil. Refer to the photo as needed.

3. Appliqué the prepared bias strips, leaves, and cherries to the border. Embroider stems for the cherries using 2 strands of green embroidery floss.

4. Referring to the following diagram, measure as indicated and make marks on the border. Draw a scalloped line connecting the marks.

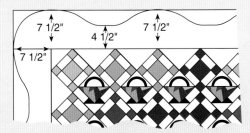

5. Layer the backing, batting, and quilt top. Baste the layers together. Baste around the quilt on the scalloped line. Quilt as desired.

6. Place the cording on the wrong side of the 7/8"-wide red bias strip. Fold the strip in half with the cording against the fold and, using a zipper foot, sew along the edge of the cording.

7. Baste the cording to the quilt, aligning the raw edge of the cording with the drawn scalloped line. Use thread to match the cording on the top and thread to match the backing in the bobbin. Overlap the cording at the ends and angle them off the quilt, as shown.

8. Trim the edge of the quilt even with the raw edge of the cording.

9. Bind the quilt using the 2 1/2"-wide black bias strips.

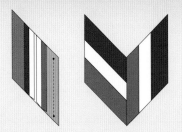

5. Set a light print square into each pair. The squares are over-sized to allow for trimming the finished block.

6. Join 2 pairs to make a half star. Join the half stars.

7. Set 4 light print triangles into the star to complete the block. Make 16 blocks.

8. Press the blocks and trim them to 9 1/2" square.

Assembly

1. Lay out the blocks in 4 rows of 4. Sew them into rows and join the rows.

2. Finish the quilt as described in the *General Directions*, using the striped bias strips for the binding.

Red Baskets

Materials

- Assorted red prints totaling at least 1/3 yard
- Assorted brown and blue prints totaling at least 1 yard
- Assorted shirting prints totaling at least 1 yard
- 1/3 yard light print for the inner border
- 1 1/2 yards red print for the outer border
- 1/2 yard green print
- 1/2 yard brown print for the binding
- 3 1/4 yards backing fabric
- 54" square of batting

Cutting

Dimensions include a 1/4" seam allowance.

For each of 4 basket blocks:
- Cut 5: 2 1/2" squares, one red print
- Cut 5: 2 1/2" squares, one shirting print
- Cut 2: 2 1/2" x 5" rectangles, same shirting print
- Cut 2: 2 3/8" squares, same shirting print, then cut them in half diagonally to yield 4 small triangles. You will use 3.
- Cut 1: 4 5/8" square, same shirting print, then cut it in half diagonally to yield 2 large triangles. You will use 1.
- Cut 1: 5 3/8" square, brown print, then cut it in half diagonally to yield 2 large triangles. You will use 1.
- Cut 1: 2 5/8" square, same brown print, then cut it in half diagonally to yield 2 small triangles
- Cut 2: 7/8" x 3 1/4" bias strips, same brown print

From the green print:
- Cut 1: 8 1/2" square
- Cut 1: 12 5/8" square, then cut it in quarters diagonally to yield 4 setting triangles
- Cut 2: 6 5/8" squares, then cut them in half diagonally to yield 4 corner triangles
- Cut 4: 3 3/4" squares, for the Star cornerstones
- Cut 4: 5 1/4" squares, green print, for the Star cornerstones

For the Sawtooth border:
- Cut 8: 5" squares, assorted red prints
- Cut 8: 5" squares, assorted shirting prints

For the Bears Paw border:
- Cut 16: 3 1/2" squares, assorted brown and blue prints
- Cut 2: 2 1/2" squares from each of the same 16 brown and blue prints
- Cut 16: 2" squares, assorted shirting prints
- Cut 2: 2 1/2" squares from each of the same 16 shirting prints
- Cut 6: 7 5/8" squares, assorted brown prints, then cut them in quarters diagonally to yield 24 setting triangles
- Cut 8: 4" squares, assorted brown prints, then cut them in half diagonally to yield 16 corner triangles

Also:
- Cut 4: 5 1/4" squares, assorted shirting prints, for the Star cornerstones
- Cut 4: 2 1/8" squares from each of the same 4 shirting prints, for the Star cornerstones
- Cut 4: 2" x 42" strips, light print

(continued on page 30)

*Elements of two different antique quilts inspired me to make **"Red Baskets."** The look I envisioned when I began this project was of a soft yet strong quilt, so I chose not to use any very dark fabrics. Arlene Martin added her beautiful hand quilting to complete its vintage charm.*

(continued from page 28)

- Cut 2: 4 1/2" x 43" lengthwise strips, red print
- Cut 2: 4 1/2" x 52" lengthwise strips, red print
- Cut 5: 2 1/2" x 42" strips, brown print

Directions

For each basket block:

1. Draw a diagonal line from corner to corner on the wrong side of each 2 1/2" shirting square.

2. Place a marked square on a 2 1/2" red print square, right sides together. Sew 1/4" away from the drawn line on both sides. Make 5.

3. Cut the squares on the drawn lines to yield 10 pieced squares. Trim the pieced squares to 2" square.

4. Lay out the pieced squares and 3 small shirting triangles, as shown. Sew them into rows and join the rows.

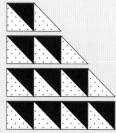

5. Sew a large brown print triangle to the unit, as shown.

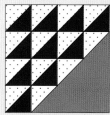

6. Press the long edges of each 7/8" x 3 1/4" brown bias strip 1/4" toward the wrong side. Trim 1/8" from the turned-under edges to reduce bulk.

7. Pin a bias strip to a 2 1/2" x 5" shirting rectangle, placing the bottom edge 1 1/4" from the bottom of the rectangle and the top edge 2" from the top. Make one and a second one reversed, as shown.

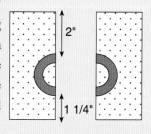

8. Sew a small brown triangle to each handle unit. NOTE: *The triangles will seem to be too small. Press the*

seam allowances toward the triangles.

9. Sew the units to the basket section. Sew a matching large shirting triangle to the bottom to complete a block. Make 4.

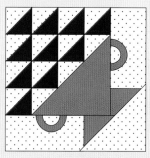

10. Referring to the photo on page 29, lay out the blocks, 8 1/2" green print square, and the green print setting and corner triangles.

11. Sew the squares and triangles into diagonal rows and join the rows.

For the Sawtooth border:

1. Draw diagonal lines from corner to corner on the wrong side of each 5" shirting square. Draw horizontal and vertical lines through the centers.

2. Place a marked shirting square on a 5" red print square, right sides together. Sew 1/4" away from the diagonal lines on both sides. Make 8.

3. Cut the squares on the drawn lines to yield 64 pieced squares. Press the seam allowances open. Trim each pieced square to 2" square.

4. Lay out 15 pieced squares, as shown. Join them to make a border. Make 2.

5. In the same manner, make 2 borders of 17 pieced squares each.

6. Sew the 15-square borders to opposite sides of the quilt. Sew the 17-square borders to the remaining sides.

For the Bears Paw border:

1. For each block make 4 matching pieced squares as

described in the basket block directions using the 2 1/2" squares. Trim each pieced square to 2" square.

2. Lay out a 3 1/2" square, 4 matching pieced squares, and the matching 2" shirting square. Sew them together to make a Bears Paw block. Make 16.

3. Lay out 4 Bears Paw blocks, 6 brown print setting triangles, and 4 brown print corner triangles. Sew them into diagonal rows and join the rows to make a border. Make 4.

For the Star cornerstones:

1. Make pieced squares as described in the Sawtooth border directions, using the 5 1/4" squares. Trim each pieced square to 2 1/8" square.

2. Lay out a 3 3/4" green print square, 8 matching pieced squares, and the matching 2 1/8" shirting squares. Sew them together to make a block. Make 4.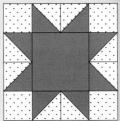

Finishing

1. Sew 2 Bears Paw borders to opposite sides of the quilt.

2. Sew the Star cornerstones to the remaining Bears Paw borders. Sew the borders to the quilt.

3. Measure the length of the quilt. Trim two 2" x 42" light print strips to that measurement. Sew them to opposite sides of the quilt.

4. Measure the width of the quilt, incuding the borders. Trim the remaining 2" x 42" light print strips to that measurement. Sew them to the remaining sides of the quilt.

5. In the same manner, trim the 4 1/2" x 43" red print strips to fit the quilt's length. Sew them to opposite sides of the quilt.

6. Trim the 4 1/2" x 52" red print strips to fit the quilt's width and sew them to the remaining sides.

7. Finish the quilt as described in the *General Directions*, using the 2 1/2" x 42" brown print strips for the binding.

General Directions

About the Patterns

Read through the pattern directions before cutting fabric. Yardage requirements are based on fabric with a useable width of 42". Pattern directions are given in step-by-step order. If you are sending your quilt to a professional machine quilter, consult the quilter regarding the necessary batting and backing size for your quilt.

Fabrics

I suggest using 100% cotton. Wash fabric in warm water with mild detergent. Do not use fabric softener. Dry fabric on a warm-to-hot setting. Press with a hot dry iron to remove any wrinkles.

Templates

Template patterns are full size and unless otherwise noted, include a 1/4" seam allowance. The solid line is the cutting line; the dashed line is the stitching line. Templates for hand piecing do not include a seam allowance.

Piecing

For machine piecing, sew 12 stitches per inch, exactly 1/4" from the edge of the fabric. To make accurate piecing easier, mark the throat plate with a piece of tape 1/4" to the right of the point where the needle pierces the fabric.

Foundation Piecing

Foundation piecing is a method for making blocks with a high degree of accuracy. Foundation patterns are full size and do not include a seam allowance. For each foundation, trace all of the lines and numbers onto paper. You will need one foundation for each block or part of a block as described in the pattern. The solid lines are stitching lines. The fabric pieces you select do not have to be cut precisely. Be generous when cutting fabric pieces as excess fabric will be trimmed away after sewing. Your goal is to cut a piece that covers the numbered area and extends into surrounding areas after seams are stitched. Generally, fabric pieces should be large enough to extend 1/2" beyond the seamline on all sides before stitching. For very small sections, or sections without angles, 1/4" may be sufficient.

Place fabric pieces on the unmarked side of the foundation and stitch on the marked side. Center the first piece, right side up, over position 1 on the unmarked side of the foundation. Hold the foundation up to a light to make sure that the raw edges of the fabric extend at least 1/2" beyond the seamline on all sides. Hold this first piece in place with a small dab of glue or a pin, as desired. Place the fabric for position 2 on the first piece, right sides together. Turn the foundation over, and sew on the line between 1 and 2, extending the stitching past the beginning and end of the line by a few stitiches on both ends. Trim the seam allowance to 1/4". Fold the position 2 piece back, right side up, and press. Continue adding pieces to the foundation in the same manner until all positions are covered and the block is complete. Trim the fabric 1/4" beyond the edge of the foundation.

To avoid disturbing the stitches, do not remove the paper until the blocks have been joined together and all the borders have been added, unless instructed to remove them sooner in the pattern. The paper will be perforated from the stitching and can be gently pulled free. Use tweezers to carefully remove small sections of the paper, if necessary.

Appliqué

Appliqué pieces can be stitched by hand or machine. To hand appliqué, baste or pin the pieces to the background in stitching order. Turn the edges under with your needle as you appliqué the pieces in place. Do not turn under or stitch edges that will be overlapped by other pieces. Finish the edges of fusible appliqué pieces with a blanket stitch made either by hand or machine.

To machine appliqué, baste pieces in place close to the edges. Then stitch over the basting with a short, wide satin stitch using a piece of tear-away stabilizer under the background fabric. You can also turn the edges of appliqué pieces under as for needleturn appliqué, and stitch them in place with a blind-hem stitch.

Pressing

Press with a dry iron. Press seam allowances toward the darker of the two pieces whenever possible. Otherwise, trim away 1/16" from the darker seam allowance to prevent it from shadowing through. Press abutting seams in opposite directions. Press all blocks, sashings, and borders before assembling the quilt top.

FINISHING YOUR QUILT
Binding

Cut the binding strips with the grain for straight-edge quilts. Binding for quilts with curved edges must be cut on the bias. To make 1/2" finished binding, cut 2 1/2"-wide strips. Sew strips together with diagonal seams; trim and press seam allowance open.

Fold the strip in half lengthwise, wrong side in, and press. Position the strip on the right side of the quilt top, aligning the raw edges of the binding with the edge of the quilt top. Leaving 6" of the binding strip free and beginning a few inches from one corner, stitch the binding to the quilt with a 1/4" seam allowance measuring from the raw edge of the quilt top. When you reach a corner, stop stitching 1/4" from the edge of the quilt top and backstitch. Clip the threads and remove the quilt from the machine. Fold the binding up and away from the quilt, forming a 45° angle, as shown.

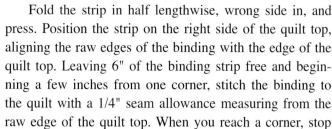

Keeping the angled fold secure, fold the binding back down. This fold should be even with the edge of the quilt top. Begin stitching at the fold.

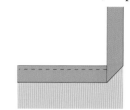

Continue stitching around the quilt in this manner to within 6" of the starting point. To finish, fold both strips back along the edge of the quilt so that the folded edges meet about 3" from both lines of the stitching and the binding lies flat on the quilt. Finger press to crease the folds. Measure the width of the folded binding. Cut the strips that distance beyond the folds. (In this case 1 1/4" beyond the folds.)

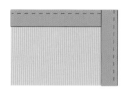

Open both strips and place the ends at right angles to each other, right sides together. Fold the bulk of the quilt out of your way. Join the strips with a diagonal seam as shown.

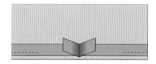

Trim the seam allowance to 1/4" and press it open. Refold the strip wrong side in. Place the binding flat against the quilt, and finish stitching it to the quilt. Trim excess batting and backing so that the binding edge will be filled with batting when you fold the binding to the back of the quilt. Blindstitch the binding to the back, covering the seamline.

Remove visible markings. Make a label that includes your name, the date the quilt was completed, and any other pertinent information, and stitch it to the back of your quilt.